Albert's Underwater ABCs

By Christopher Straub

A is for Alligator

B is for

Barnacles

C is for

Clownfish

D is for

Dugong

E is for

Eel

F is for

Flying Fish

G is for

Giant Squid

H is for

Horseshoe Crab

I is for

Indian
Sea Star

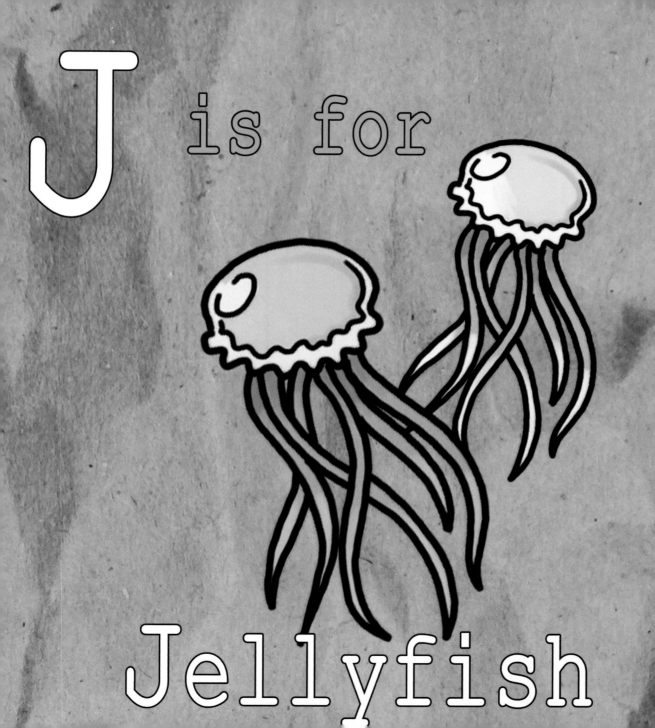

J is for

Jellyfish

K is for

Kelp

L

is for

Lobster

M is for

Manatee

N is for Narwhal

O is for

Octopus

P is for

Pufferfish

Q is for

Queen Conch

R is for

Ray

S is for

Shark

T is for

Turtle

U is for

Urchin

V is for

Vampire Squid

W is for

Walrus

X is for

X-Ray Tetra

Y is for

Yellowfin Tuna

Z is for

Zooplankton

Albert the Confused Manatee Book and Plush Toy
Available at www.ConfusedManatee.com